COMMON CORE CLINICS

Grade 2

English Language Arts

CLINICS

Foundational Skills

Common Core Clinics, English Language Arts, Foundational Skills, Grade 2
OT210 / 462NA

ISBN-13: 978-0-7836-8579-3

Cover Image: © Kudryashka/Veer

Triumph Learning® 136 Madison Avenue, 7th Floor, New York, NY 10016

© 2012 Triumph Learning, LLC
Coach is an imprint of Triumph Learning®

The National Governors Association Center for Best Practices and Council of Chief State School Officers are the sole owners and developers of the Common Core State Standards, © Copyright 2010. All rights reserved.

ALL ABOUT YOUR BOOK

COMMON CORE CLINICS will help you master important reading skills.

Get the Idea
teaches you a skill.

Think About It
gives you help
while you practice.

Read Aloud with the class
to use your
new skills.

Try It!
lets you practice
on your own.

Table of Contents

Lesson 1 Words with Short Vowels

Get the Idea

 A vowel usually makes the **short vowel sound** if there is one vowel in a short word. Short vowels can be spelled <u>a</u>, <u>e</u>, <u>i</u>, <u>o</u>, or <u>u</u>.

a   clam

e   belt

Circle the words with short vowel sounds.

crash	cave	flame	flash
shell	cheek	chest	keep

🍎 A short vowel word can be spelled with **consonants** at the beginning and end of the word. The vowel can be in the middle.

i   drip

o   pot

u   brush

• •

Circle the words with short vowel sounds.

fill	file	flock	code
flute	crust	thin	clog

Think About It

★ Say each word. Listen to the vowel sound.

Draw a line from the short vowel to the matching picture.

a

e

i

o

u

6

★ Say each word. Listen to the sound between consonants.

Circle the words with a short vowel sound.

sock

clap

grapes

bone

plum

desk

Try It!

Which word has the short **e** sound? Circle it.

stem   stop   key

• •

Which word has the short **i** sound? Circle it.

ice   lid   stump

8

Read Aloud

Read the story. Draw a picture about the story in the box. Write a sentence about your picture.

Trip on a Step

My mom came home with milk. My mom tripped on the front step. She did not fall or get hurt. But she dropped the milk. It spilled on the ground. Some cats licked it up. Mom went back to the store to get more milk.

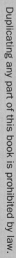

Lesson 2 Words with Long Vowels

Get the Idea

A **long vowel sound** sounds like the letter that stands for it. Long vowels can be <u>a</u>, <u>e</u>, <u>i</u>, <u>o</u>, <u>u</u>, and sometimes <u>y</u>. Sometimes a word with a long vowel sound ends with a silent <u>e</u>.

a   plate

o   bone

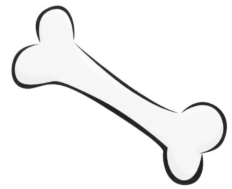

Circle the words with long vowel sounds.

gate	sack	shine	drill
hose	chop	mule	thumb

10

🍎 Sometimes a word with a long **i** sound does not end with a silent <u>e</u>.

i   s**i**gn

🍎 The letter <u>y</u> can make a long **i** sound.

y   cr**y**

fl**y**

Circle the words with long vowel sounds.

blind   pint   mind   spin

fry   dry   yes   yell

Think About It

★ The letter y can stand for a long i sound.

Draw a line from the long vowel to the matching picture.

a

e

y

o

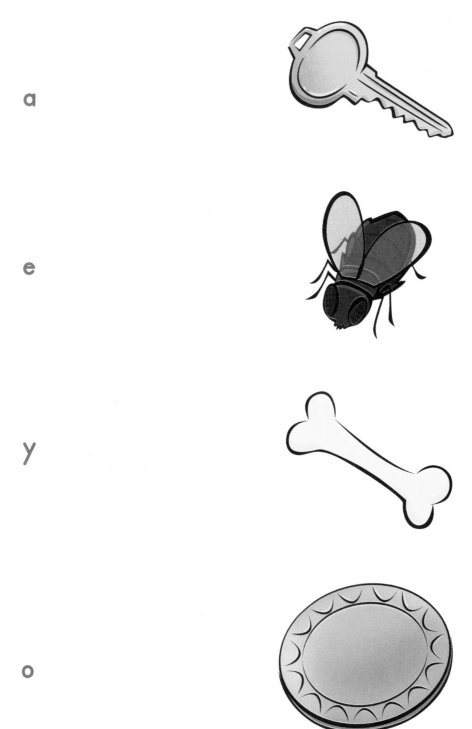

★ Some words with a long vowel sound end with a silent <u>e</u>.

Make a check ✓ next to the words with a long vowel sound.

_____ belt

_____ clam

_____ bone

_____ brush

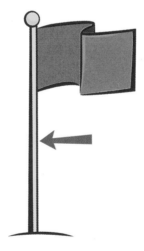

_____ pole

_____ fly

Try It!

Which word has the long **a** sound? Circle it.

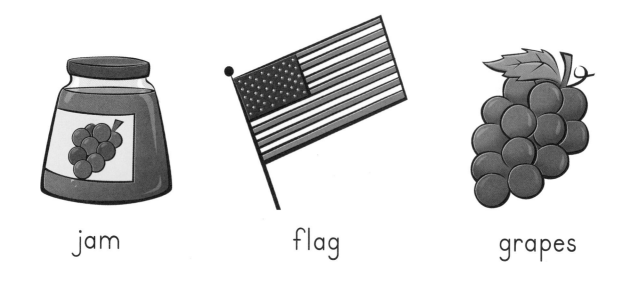

jam   flag   grapes

• •

Which word has the long **o** sound? Circle it.

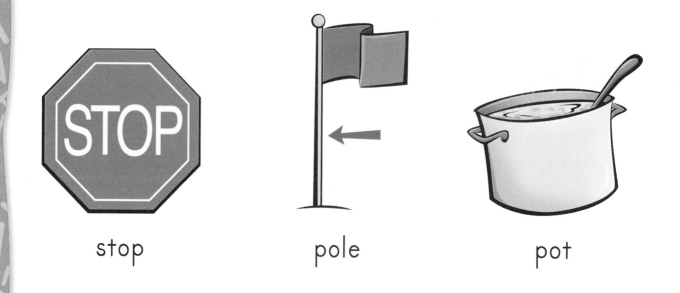

stop   pole   pot

14

Read Aloud

Read the story. Draw a picture about the story in the box. Write a sentence about your picture.

My Grape Plate

Dad broke my new plate. I was sad. I liked that plate a lot. There was art of grapes on it. I wanted him to fix it with tape. He said it could not be fixed. He said he would buy me a new one.

Lesson 3 Words with Vowel Teams

Get the Idea

🍎 Two **vowels** can work together to make one vowel sound in a **vowel team**. The letters **oa** stand for the long **o** sound.

oa   loaf

🍞 The letters **ea** can stand for the long **e** sound.

ea   wheat

Circle the words with long vowel teams.

boat	goal	doll	crop
team	steam	stem	spend

16

🍎 Vowel teams can come in the middle of a word.

snail  seed

🍎 Vowel teams can come at the end of a word.

blue  toe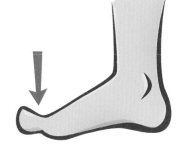

Circle the words with long vowel teams.

trail	hail	tree	stamp	green
clue	true	doe	bond	hoe

Think About It

★ Vowel teams stand for long vowel sounds. Some vowel teams come at the end of words.

Draw a line from the vowel team to the matching picture.

e e

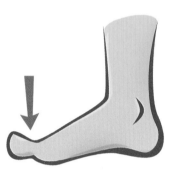

o a

a i

o e

18

★ A vowel team has two vowels next to each other that make one sound.

Make a check ✔ next to the words that have a vowel team.

_____ blue

_____ wheat

_____ bone

_____ daisy

_____ stream

_____ desk

19

Try It!

Which words have a vowel team? Circle them.

stream   wheat   grapes

braid   tree   cube

20

Read Aloud Read the story. Draw a picture about the story in the box. Write a sentence about your picture.

Blue Pail

I have a blue pail I use to keep rocks. I look for rocks in the green grass in my yard. I see a rock by my toe. I go to pick it up. It is not a rock. It is a snail. I leave it alone and keep looking for rocks.

Lesson 4 Words with Two Syllables

Get the Idea

A **two-syllable word** has two vowel sounds. Each **syllable** in a two-syllable word has one **vowel** sound.

baby   **ba / by**

behind   **be / hind**

Circle the words with two syllables.

gravy   grass   bean   below

chimney   chirp   feather   lawn

Two-syllable words can have a **vowel team**.

daisy   dai / sy

 A syllable can have one letter or many letters.

apron   a / pron

Circle the words with two syllables.

teacher	raisin	school	house
brass	erase	labor	pound

Think About It

★ A syllable needs a vowel sound.

Color one 🙂 next to the word for each syllable in the word.

remote 🙂 🙂

clover 🙂 🙂

peanut 🙂 🙂

bench 🙂 🙂

bacon 🙂 🙂

cube 🙂 🙂

24

★ Say each word. Count the syllables on your fingers.

Make a check ✓ next to the words that have two syllables.

_____ tulip

_____ plum

_____ cherry

_____ clam

_____ beaver

_____ honey

Try It!

Which words have two syllables? Circle them.

rainbow

penny

thread

cherry

chimney

bench

Read Aloud

Read the story. Draw a picture about the story in the box. Circle the words with two syllables. Write a sentence about your picture.

Lucky Things

Some people believe some things can bring good luck. A clover and a rainbow may be lucky. Some say a horseshoe is lucky. Other people think wishing on a shooting star brings good luck. I think a tulip and a penny are lucky, too.

Lesson 5 Irregular Word Sounds

Get the Idea

🍎 Some words are spelled the same way but sound different. The same letters can work together in different words to stand for different sounds. The letters **ea** can stand for the long **e** sound.

e a   j e a n s

🍎 The letters **ea** can stand for the short **e** sound.

e a   t h r e a d

Circle the words that use **ea** as a short **e** sound.

head	bread	clean	mean
heat	steam	spread	measure

28

Some letters do not match the sounds they make.
The letters **gh** can be silent.

sleig**h**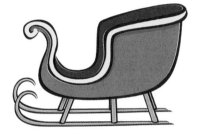

dou**gh**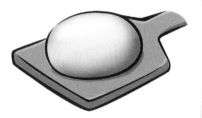

The letters **gh** can stand for the **f** sound.

cou**gh**

lau**gh**

Circle the words that use **gh** to stand for the **f** sound. Draw a line under the words that have a silent **gh**.

though	rough	high	thigh
tough	sigh	through	laugh

Think About It

⭐ Sometimes **gh** can be silent. Sometimes **gh** can stand for the **f** sound.

Circle the words where **gh** stands for the **f** sound.

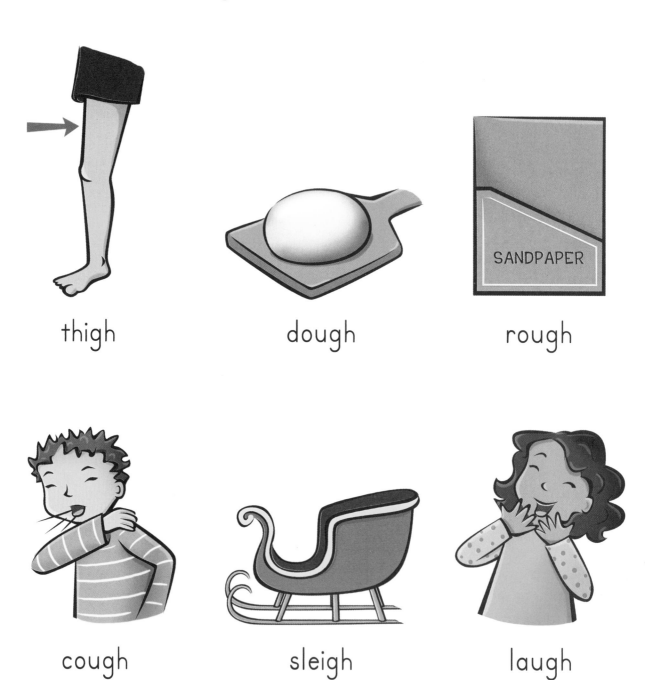

thigh

dough

rough

cough

sleigh

laugh

★ The letters **ea** can stand for a long **e** sound or a short **e** sound.
Circle the words where **ea** stands for the short **e** sound.

beak	bread	peanut

stream	thread	spread

Try It!

In which word is **gh** silent? Circle it.

rough   sleigh   laugh

Which word with **ea** has a short **e** sound? Circle it.

jeans   beaver   breath

32

Read Aloud

Read the story. Draw a picture about the story in the box. Write a sentence about your picture.

Rough Day at the Beach

I do not like the beach. The sand feels rough on my skin. The sand gets onto our clothes and food. Dad brings bread for us to eat. We do not get to eat it, though. Seagulls come and steal our bread. Then, they fly away up high. That is enough for me.

Lesson 6 Prefixes

Get the Idea

A **prefix** is a word part that is added to the beginning of a **base word**. The prefix changes the meaning of the base word.

The prefix **un-** means "not."

un- + happy   **un**happy

The prefix **re-** means "again."

re- + use   **re**use

Draw a line under the words that have a prefix that means "not." Circle the words that have a prefix that means "again."

unclean	unpack	reread	rewrite
reattach	retest	unfair	unbuckled

34

🍎 The prefix **mis-** means "wrong."

mis- + spell   **mis**spell

The prefix **pre-** means "before."

pre- + school   **pre**school

Draw a line under the words that have a prefix that means "wrong." Circle the words that have a prefix that means "before."

misspeak   preheat   predawn   mismatch

preplan   preview   mislead   misprint

35

Think About It

⭐ A prefix can be added to the beginning of a word.

Draw a line from the prefix to a word next to a picture to make a new word.

mis-   clean

un-   step

pre-   paint

re-   heat

36

⭐ The prefix **un-** means "not." The prefix **mis-** means "wrong."

Add a prefix to each word.

_____tied

_____pack

_____spell

_____count

Try It!

Which word has a prefix? Circle the prefix.

miscount   mirror   messy

• •

Which word means "use again"? Circle it.

reuse   reed   rest

My Pretest Mistake

I took a spelling pretest. I made a few mistakes. I was unhappy. I have to review a spelling list. Then, I will do better on the real test. If I do poorly on the test, my teacher will let me take a retest.

Lesson 7 Suffixes

Get the Idea

🍎 A **suffix** is a word part that is added to the end of a **base word**. A suffix changes the meaning of the base word.

🍎 The suffix **-less** means "without."

care + -less   careless

🍎 The suffix **-ful** means "full of."

help + -ful   helpful

• •

Draw a line under the suffix that means "without." Circle the suffix that means "full of."

hopeless	joyful	playful	shoeless
fearless	careful	painless	useful

40

The suffix **-ly** means "in a way."

slow + **-ly**   slow**ly**

 The suffix **-ness** means "a way to be or feel."

sweet + **-ness**   sweet**ness**

Underline the suffix that means "in a way." Circle the suffix that means "a way to be or feel."

quickly   sadness   shyly   happiness

gladly   goodness   badly   freshness

Think About It

★ A suffix can be added to the end of a word.

Draw a line from the suffix to the word next to the picture to make a new word.

-less   glad

-ful   quiet

-ness   hat

-ly   pain

42

⭐ The suffix **-less** means "without." The suffix **-ness** means "a way to be or feel."

Add a suffix to each word.

shoe_____

glad_____

sad_____

fear_____

43

Try It!

Which word has a suffix? Circle the suffix.

loudly   wagon   cold

· ·

Which word means "full of play"? Circle it.

walk   playful   cherry

44

Read Aloud

Read the story. Draw a picture about the story in the box. Circle the suffixes in the story. Write a sentence about your picture.

Joyful Hal

Hal was feeling joyful. It was a cloudless day. Hal ran shoeless in his yard. He sang loudly and playfully. His mother was amused by his happiness.

Lesson 8 Words with Silent Letters

Get the Idea

Some words have silent letters. These words have letters that do not stand for sounds you hear when you say the words. You can use a **dictionary** to check how to spell and read a word.

comb

sign

island

Circle the words that have silent letters.

lamb	lamp	aisle	raisin
climb	club	sign	dump

46

🍎 Some words begin with a silent **k**.

knee 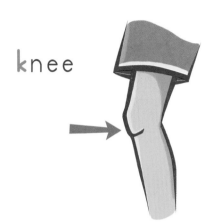 knot

🍎 The letters **gh** can be silent in the middle of a word.

kni**gh**t  li**gh**t

Circle the words that start with a silent **k**.

keep   knife   king   know

Think About It

★ Some words have silent letters at the end.

Color the 🙂 next to the words that end with a silent **b**.

climb

bib

comb

club

job

lamb

48

⭐ Silent letters can come in the middle of a word.

Make a check ✔ next to the words that have silent letters.

____ island

____ plum

____ sign

____ knight

____ light

____ belt

Try It!

Which words start with a silent **k**? Circle them.

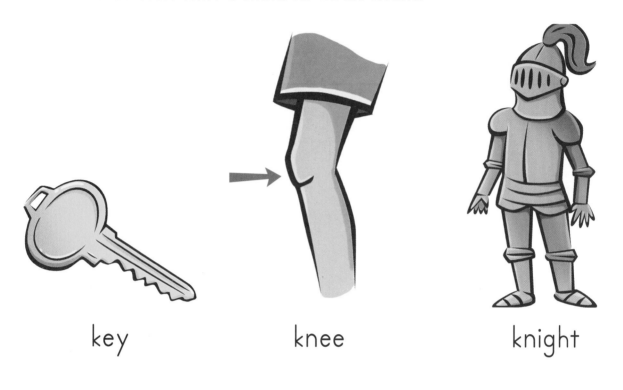

key   knee   knight

Which words end with a silent **b**? Circle them.

lamb   club   comb

50

Read Aloud Read the story. Draw a picture about the story in the box. Write a sentence about your picture.

The Knight, the Comb, and the Lamb

There was a knight who lived on an island. His favorite thing to do was to comb his curly hair until it was straight. He would comb it day and night. One day he found a lamb. He liked the lamb's curly hair. He thought he would like to have curly hair, too. He threw his comb away.

Glossary

B

base word

a word that stands alone and can have word parts added to it (Lessons 6 and 7)

Example: happy

C

consonant

any letter that is not a vowel (Lesson 1)

Example: B,C,D

D

dictionary

a book of words that shows how to spell each word and what it means (Lesson 8)

L

long vowel sound

a vowel sound that sounds like the name of the letter that stands for it (Lesson 2)

Example: gate

P

prefix

a word part added to the beginning of a base word that changes the meaning of the base word

(Lesson 6)

Example: The prefix <u>un-</u> means "not."
The prefix <u>re-</u> means "again."

S

short vowel sound

a vowel sound that does not sound like the name
of the letter (Lesson 1)

> Example: the sound of *a* as in clap

suffix

a word part added to the end of a base
word (Lesson 7)

> Example: The suffix <u>–less</u> means "without."
> The suffix <u>–ful</u> means "full of."

syllable

a word part with one vowel sound (Lesson 4)

T

two-syllable word

a word with two parts (Lesson 4)

    Example: The word <u>pretend</u> has two syllables:

          pre / tend
            1   2

V

vowel

a, e, i, o, u, and sometimes y (Lessons 3 and 4)

vowel team

two vowels that work together to make one sound (Lessons 3 and 4)

    Example: heal

Fun and Games

Long Vowel, Short Vowel

How to play:

1. Cut out the picture cards on page 57.
2. Place cards face down in a pile.
3. Invite a partner to play. Choose a card from the pile. Say the name of the picture on the card.
4. Your partner says if the name has a long vowel sound or a short vowel sound.
5. The game ends when all the vowel sounds have been named.
6. Shuffle the cards and switch places to repeat the game.

Guess Who I Am

How to play:

1. Cut out the picture cards on page 59.
2. Place cards face down in a pile.
3. Invite a partner to play. Choose a card from the pile. Describe the card to your partner. He or she tries to guess the picture on the card.
4. You can give clues to describe the card. One clue should tell something about the word. Other clues can tell about the picture. For example: I have two syllables. I end in **y**. I am a very young person. Answer: **baby**.
5. Take turns until all the pictures have been described and guessed.

Make a Sentence

How to play:

1. Cut out the cards on page 63.
2. Shuffle the cards.
3. Invite a partner to play. Deal each player 10 cards, face down.
4. Look at your cards to pair a noun with a verb. Take turns saying a sentence using each pair. Then put the pairs in a pile.
5. Choose a noun or verb from the cards left in your hand.
6. Ask your partner for a card to make a pair.
   For example: I have a noun. Do you have a verb?
7. If your partner has the right card, he or she should give it to you. Then try to use the pair in a sentence. If you can make a sentence, you can keep the pair.
8. Take turns until all the cards are matched.

woman	pony	lion	mother
father	rabbit	child	clown
actor	doctor	runs	sings
dances	jumps	laughs	cries
helps	thinks	sneezes	works